the
DALÍ
universe

By Beniamino Levi

This publication accompanies the exhibition
The Dalí Universe
located at County Hall, Riverside Building, London
Organised by The Stratton Foundation
Curator: Beniamino Levi

In association with

THE 🏛 TIMES

Printed in Italy by:
Società editrice Umberto Allemandi & C.
Text and Documentation Editors:
Kathryn Tomasetti and Antonia Spanos
Cover photo: © Robert Whittaker
ISBN: 88-422-0990-2

CONTENTS

THE DALÍ UNIVERSE

Beniamino Levi
President, The Stratton Foundation
Curator, *The Dalí Universe*

I have been given the great honour of curating a new and exciting Salvador Dalí exhibition for the County Hall Gallery, the newest cultural centre in one of the most important and cosmopolitan cities in the world...London...known for its established culture and as a leader in developing new trends. As President of The Stratton Foundation, an organisation dedicated to the enrichment of the cultural arts, I have curated over 60 Dalí shows throughout the world, in major international museums. *The Dalí Universe* in London will feature a large grouping of various rare artworks, selected from private collections and cultural organisations throughout the world, including sculpture, artglass, collages, gold *objets d'art*, furniture, and rare graphic portfolios, most of which have never been seen before in Britain.

This exhibition is intended to reveal the foundations that lay beneath Salvador Dalí's inspired genius, and to offer an understanding of his art and life. It will allow the visitor to delve into the labyrinth of Dalí's mind and to view the creative results of his infinite imagination. For me, it is the culmination of many years of admiration, astonishment and involvement in the Surreal world of Dalí.

My own adventure as a Dalí collector, as well as my relationship with Salvador Dalí himself, started in the late 1960s. At the time I was in the process of organising a Surrealist exhibition at my art gallery in Milan, focusing on the more prominent artists who took part in the movement during the 1920s and 1930s, as well as those who were strongly influenced by this movement. I had managed to collect paintings by Ernst, Picabia, Lam, Matta, Magritte, Masson, De Chirico and many others. Unfortunately, I was unable to locate any works by Salvador Dalí for my exhibition. No Surrealist exhibition would make sense without the works of the Catalan genius, because without the inclusion of Dalí, the show would have been incomplete both historically and artistically. Dalí was a defining entity in establishing the theory of Surrealism:

"The only difference between Surrealism and myself is that I am Surrealism."

An artist is not one who is inspired,
but one who can inspire others

Dalí, among all the Surrealists, was the only one who constantly lived and implemented the principles of Surrealism in his life.

I left for Paris in order to meet Dalí, and to buy some of his paintings, hoping to acquire those which would be most representative of his style. I must admit that I was both excited and worried at the prospect of meeting such a renowned artist. The crucial meeting changed my life personally and professionally. It took place at the famed Maurice Hotel where Dalí used to spend four months a year. (The rest of the year he usually divided between New York and Spain).

Our meeting was extraordinary and exceeded all my expectations. What struck me immediately was his egocentric personality. Dalí was extremely curious as to my interest in him and began a seemingly endless monologue, which I was totally powerless to stop. He

spoke French, stressing and emphasising some words in Spanish, his mother tongue. His speech ranged over many fields: astronomy, art, philosophy and mathematics with no apparent logic and seemingly based entirely on a purely imaginative level. Despite feeling overwhelmed, I was fascinated by the strength of his ideas and his charismatic yet theatrical antics. After some reflection, I realised that his apparently senseless monologue had meaning only when filtered through the "sensors" of rationalised irrationality. That first meeting made a lasting impression both in my mind and in my heart.

After that day, and after the exhibition, I did not have the chance to meet with Dalí until several years later. The meeting took place in the same Maurice Hotel in Paris, and was held in order to discuss my dealings in his work. Having positive results, our strange relationship grew stronger. During the 1970s many other meetings followed, both in Paris and in his house in Cadaqués, Spain. During the course of these encounters, I noticed some sculptures located in the studio where our meetings took place. I thought these were the same sculptures Dalí had described as those he created when he was alone and wanted to relax from the obsessive and hallucinatory tensions that bothered him frequently during the day. I knew that his attitude towards the sculptural form was both scientific and metamorphic. He had spoken often with me on the subject. The following, taken from his autobiography, *La Vie Secrète de Salvador Dalí*, reveals his true thoughts:

"Nowadays we know that shape always results from an inquisitive process of the material...the specific reaction of the material when submitted to the terrible coercive strength of space that stifles it, pressing and squeezing it all over. Until it creates those swellings that, bouncing from its life, reach the precise limits established by the rigorous outlines of its own original reaction. Many times a piece of material pushed by a exceedingly absolute impulse has been denied; while another piece of material manages to create its own particular life, a piece of material that tries to be what it is possible for it to be, abandoning itself to the pleasure of creating new shapes, despite the tyrannical impact of space."

It was very impressive. I asked Dalí and his secretary whether I could buy the sculptures I had seen, and I urged Dalí to create more. It was in this way that I began to collect Salvador Dalí's sculpture on behalf of private collectors. I began to search all over the world for other sculpture that he had created in the past. Tracking these sculptures down in Surrealist exhibition cata-

logues, I was able to locate many artworks created and exhibited by Dalí throughout his illustrious career. My research was thrilling and exhausting. Ultimately it resulted in a major Dalí sculptural collection that is now the most important of its kind in the world.

THE EXHIBIT

For the London show, I have chosen to display Dalí's artworks within the three major themes that best represent Dalí's artistic legacy; "Dreams & Fantasy", "Sensuality & Femininity", and "Religion & Mythology". I have carefully selected the works which will be displayed, drawing

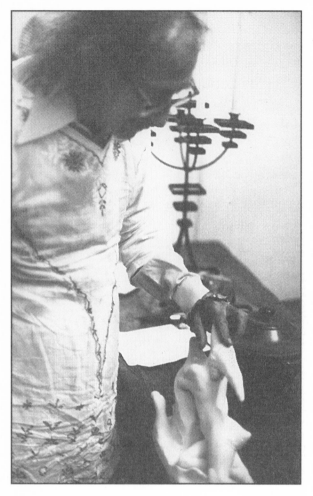

from private collections and cultural foundations the world over. As all artists tend to work thematically, it is only through complete involvement and immersion in these ideas that one may grow to understand and truly appreciate each artist's output. My goal is to exhibit exactly the right art which best represents these three ideas, therefore rendering the exhibition infrastructure both educational and exciting for the London public. Included in the art that I have chosen are rare portfolios of graphics illustrating the great themes of literature, *pâte de verre* sculptures created in collaboration with the famed French crystallerie Daum, furniture designed in the 1930s in Paris, golden *objets d'art* inspired by jewellery from the court of Louis XIV, the painting commissioned by Alfred Hitchcock for his 1945 Hollywood blockbuster "Spellbound", and countless other examples of Dalí's wide artistic range. *The Dalí Universe* also features specially created nocturnal passages, interspersed with music, light, Dalí's own voice, and various special effects. The visitor is offered a Surreal world, a chance to enter into Dalí's imagination, and a total re-creation of a true Dalinean atmosphere; all right in the heart of London.

My experience with Dalí has been a lifelong adventure, and I am secure in the knowledge that it is a relationship that will continue to enthral me for the rest of my life. I am more than delighted to accept the honour that has been bestowed on me to curate *The Dalí Universe* at London's County Hall. With artworks amassed from around the world, in order to honour Dalí's artistic legacy, I feel Dalí's genius will be apparent to those who attend the show. Most importantly, rather than an average museum exhibit, *The Dalí Universe* will be a total Dalí experience – an immersion into the wild and vibrant imagination of Salvador Dalí. I hope that the audience in Britain will be as captivated by Dalí as I still am today, many years after my first encounter with the great Surrealist Master.

THE PRIVILEGE OF WORKING WITH DALÍ

Enric Sabater i Bonany
Andorra, March 2000

"Do not fear perfection, you will never achieve it."
Salvador Dalí- *Diary of a Genius*

The organisers of the *Dalí Universe* exhibition at County Hall in London have asked me to write a few lines for the catalogue, on no better grounds than having worked with the artist as his personal secretary and, if I may say so, as a friend and close collaborator for over twelve years. Although I am writing this far from London, the name of the city conjures up all my memories of the great Salvador Dalí retrospective exhibition there (which came from the Centre Georges Pompidou in Paris) just twenty years ago, to which I devoted much time and effort.

In tracing the itineraries of Dalí life, we start with Figueras (the town in Catalonia where he was born, where his museum is located and where he is at rest forever), Cadaqués (where he lived and had his only home), Paris for the obligatory annual visit, and the St. Regis Hotel in New York.

It is often forgotten that artistic circles in Britain have always been especially sensitive to Dalí's work. Some forty years ago the Glasgow Art Gallery, for example, exhibited his *Christ of St. John of the Cross*, a key work in Dalí's religious phase and now included in the exhibition "Seeing Salvation: The Image of Christ" currently being held at the National Gallery. This provides us with a link to the first section of *The Dalí Universe*: "Religion and Mythology".

It should be remembered that Salvador Dalí was born, educated, married and died within the Catholic Church. But at the same time he was a profoundly Mediterranean man. While he painted his Madonnas- the one in *The Ecumenical Council* (1960), *The Madonna of Port Lligat* (in several versions), the memorable oil painting of *The Last Supper* (1955), the extraordinary *Corpus Hypercubus* (1954)- and his *St. James the Great* (1957), nonetheless mythological deities appear regularly in his art: Narcissus, Bacchus and Venus, among others. In fact, we would find it hard to understand Dalí disassociated from the Mediterranean settings of the great mythologies- the Egyptian, the Greek and the Latin- and of the great monotheistic

religions- Judaism, Christianity and Islam. The Jewish and Muslim religions were both present in his work, albeit the less well known parts of it.

The second section of the exhibition is described as "Sensuality and Femininity". This subject was clearly a constant source of inspiration in Dalí's art. Strangely enough, many years passed before he painted the most sensual portraits of his wife Gala: *Galarina* (1945) and several earlier studies, *My wife, Nude, Contemplating Her Own Flesh Becoming Stairs, Three Vertebrae of a Column, Sky and Architecture* (1945) and *Leda Atomica* (1949), the year in which Gala posed as the model for the first version of *The Madonna of Port Lligat.*

Dalí alternated his religious themes with others of a purely sensual nature, where the subject matter extended also to erotica. Luis Romero, an expert of Dalí's work, says the compositions of this type are *"the other side of the coin of his mystical images; they must be considered as one of the many trips down to the hell of secret exaltations which, according to custom, are manifested in a fairly public way"*. And Fleur Cowles confirms this when she writes: *"Nobody has led a more public private life than Dalí"*. His concept of the feminine ideal was identified solely with the figure of Gala, as he himself admitted: *"I burnished Gala in order to make her shine, making her as happy as possible. And I took greater care of her than of myself, for without her everything would have come to an end."* I can personally attest to this constancy. Shortly after I stopped working with Dalí, Gala died and the artist began his steady decline. His feminine ideal had disappeared, and without it Dalí faded away. They had lived together for fifty-two years, which is an entire lifetime.

The organisers of the exhibition, The Stratton Foundation, tell me they are devoting a section to "Dreams and Fantasy". Was Dalí a dreamer? Did he get carried away by fantasies? To me it certainly seemed so during those years I was with him, although in his *Diary of a Genius* he shows little inclination to believe in fantasy; rather the opposite, for he writes: *"Every morning, when I wake up I experience an exquisite joy that I had not altogether realised until now - the joy of being Salvador Dalí."*

Quite another thing is the fact that certain critics have wished to see only exaggerated fantasy and interpretations of dreams in Dalí' s work, possibly because of his interest in figures and in the work of Sigmund Freud- he painted an excellent portrait of the psychoanalyst in 1937 and several others relating to the father of psychoanalysis in 1938- and the drawings to illustrate *The Secret Life of Salvador Dalí*. On the other hand, what I can certify is that Dalí was always an indefatigable worker, tenacious and persistent (little inclined to fantasy, according to him), and totally devoted to constant creativity. Disciplined and strict, whether he was in Port Lligat, Paris or New York, he kept to his "working hours" with splendid results. *"As Salvador Dalí grew older, he became more serious, more orderly, more pensive"*, wrote Josep Pla in *Obres de Museu*, for the writer knew Dalí intimately, both as a person and as an artist.

There comes a moment in every person's life when they realize they adore me

The result of all this is the dimension of Salvador Dalí's oeuvre. It will possibly require the work of several generations of experts and critics in order to understand it, and even then only approximately so.

What I hope and wish for this exhibition, for whose organisers, The Stratton Foundation, I have great respect, is that it responds to the high standards they set in those previously shown in cities such as Rome, Berlin and Milan, and that visitors will be able to obtain a better understanding of this unique, unrepeatable artist with whom I had the privilege to work for over a dozen unforgettable years. As I wrote in my first book, *To Sabater with best wishes, on the Queen Elisabeth, Dalí: "They were twelve years filled with adventure, with happiness and sadness, perhaps the hardest, most complicated and tempestuous years of my life, and certainly the most fascinating."*

SALVADOR DALÍ: ENIGMA, PROVOCATEUR, ENFANT TERRIBLE

Ralf Michler
Dalí Expert and Inventory of Works Author

"I am perfectly aware that my enemies, my friends, and the public generally protest that they do not understand the meaning of the emerging images that I transform into my paintings. And yet, how are they supposed to understand me, since even myself, their "creator", do not understand them? The fact that I myself, in the act of painting, do not understand the meaning of my paintings does not mean that they have no meaning: on the contrary, their meaning is so inscrutable, so complex, so coherent, and so involuntary, that it is beyond the simple analysis of logical thought."

DALÍ AS ENIGMA?

All through his life, Salvador Dalí loved to shock and to irritate the world around him. He was a man of many faces, who perhaps always remained a mystery even to himself. As one of the pioneers of surrealism he was at once author, stage designer, jeweller, filmmaker, book illustrator, graphic artist, and "craftsman" - a man who sought to express his surrealist principles in three-dimensional form. This is best illustrated by the sculpture "Woman in Flames", a combination of 2 Dalí ideas: both fire, the hidden intensity of unconscious desire, and the female figure with drawers, which represents small, hidden secrets. His ideas and associations made him as famous as his works did. So it is hardly surprising that even at the age of seven he had declared his intention to become a genius. This early statement of intent should also be seen in terms of his confrontational relationship with his very considerate and dutiful mother, and his free-thinking, domineering father, a lawyer in Figueras. Dalí had come to feel early that the "provocative love" of his parents was directed not just at him, but also at his brother, who had died at just two years of age, in 1903.

"I felt that desire to become another I, with that violence and intensity that is allowed in the symbiotic and undifferentiated world of the first years of one's life. On the borders of this swirling chasm, I constructed the gelatinous fortress of paranoia, whose craggy parapet was the immense presence, the formidable strength of my father...although later he repelled me, I retained him within me, filled with reverence for the strength of his personality, because I needed his weight, his density, as a support for the interior of my flowing mental structures."

So Dalí developed early the ability to transform his conflicts into strengths and to cultivate them as fertile ground for his paintings. Again and again, he attempted to overcome the overpowering father figure, so that he was later gratified to find confirmation in Freud that the true hero is he who succeeds in rebelling against the authority of his father, in order to dethrone him[2].

WAS DALÍ REALLY AN ENIGMA TO HIMSELF OR TO US?

Salvador Dalí would later describe his elaborately cultivated moustache as a pair of antennae, which were able to receive cosmic vibrations. As a painter he became famous for pictures such as *The Persistence of Memory,* painted in 1931. The

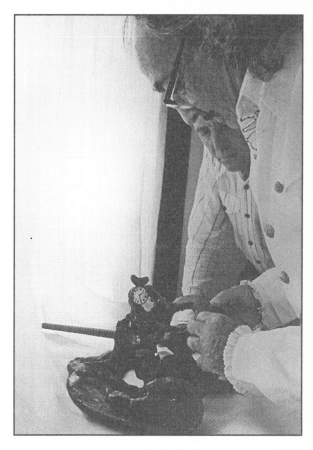

melting, overripe Camembert clocks were intended as a visual representation of Einstein's concept of space and time. The detailed accuracy of his technique always made his pictures seem like photographs.

Dalí first studied art in Madrid, in the 1920s. After inciting his fellow students to protest, he found himself banned from studying for a year. In 1924, he was finally obliged to leave the Academy of Art, after explaining that he had not appeared for an examination because his teachers were not capable of judging his work.

DALÍ AS PROVOCATEUR?

In 1939, Dalí designed two windows for Bonwit-Teller in New York. When they were altered without his knowledge, he smashed one of the window panes in anger, and as a result was held in custody for a while at a police station. A similar event occurred after his pavilion design for the Amusement Park at the New York World's Fair was not carried out according to his instructions. In protest he designed a leaflet imitating the American Constitution: the "Declaration of Independence of the Imagination and Declaration of Man's Right to His Insanity"[3]. Later in his life, Dalí said of himself: *"The only difference between me and a madman - I'm not mad. I am because I'm mad, and I'm mad - because I am."*

In the early 1940s, Dalí designed his first pieces of jewellery, worked on the ballet *Labyrinth,* and worked on his autobiography *The Secret Life of Salvador Dalí,* which was published in

New York in 1942. The cover for his exhibition at Julien Levy in New York shows his *Soft self-portrait with Cooked Bacon,* which Dalí would later describe as an "anti-psychological self-portrait":

"Rather than painting the soul, the inside, I paint the outside, the outer casing, the glove of my Self...I am the most noble of all painters, and as such I issue a permanent invitation to dine, thus providing delicious nourishment for our age"[4].

DALÍ AS ENFANT TERRIBLE?

In a tabular sketch entitled *Polifacetic Dalí,* he describes himself in turn as mystic, philosopher, architect, jeweller, inventor, show master, theorist, novelist, stage designer, librettist, filmmaker, sculptor, and painter. The term "show master" is a reference to the public appearances that he had been giving, as veritable "happenings", since the 1930s. In 1936 he made the introductory speech at the Surrealism exhibition wearing a diving suit, and in 1954, in Rome, he emerged from a giant egg, which he called the "metaphysical cube", to declare that he had been reborn.

These appearances were clearly deliberate attempts to attract media attention to himself. Dalí, just like Warhol in later years, was one of the first artists to use publicity as a means of communicating his artistic message. He thus understood early on how television worked and the astonishingly powerful effect it could have on the masses. The Dalí myth that he himself created, which he once described as his greatest work of art, and which he constantly embellished, whether in his autobiographical writing or in his various interviews, created such a climate of expectation that he was forced into playing a role that he could no longer escape and that certainly became a burden to him in his later life. Close friends recounted how Dalí would be perfectly sincere and unpretentious among friends, but as soon as strangers arrived, or a camera appeared, his behaviour would change entirely, and he would enter into a "pose". At such moments he would whisper to his friends: *"Maintenant je dois faire du Dalí"* (I have to play Dalí now)[5].

Thus did Dalí gradually transform himself into a media event, independently of his art, with the result that 85% of all Germans have some idea who Salvador Dalí was - a level of fame

For me, love must be ugly, looks must be divine, and death must be beautiful

that many television stars can only dream of. In his *Diary of a Genius*, Dalí writes:

"Every morning when I wake up, I feel an exquisite sense of joy - the joy of being Salvador Dalí. And I ask myself, in a sort of rapture, what wonderful thing will he create today, this Salvador Dalí. And as every day passes, I find it harder and harder to understand how other people can possibly bear to exist without being Salvador Dalí."

Asked about his life, Dalí said:

"At the age of three, I wanted to be a female cook (he gave particular stress to the word female). At seven, Napoleon. After that, my ambition just went on growing. I wanted to be Salvador Dalí and nobody else. And yet, the nearer I come to my goal, the farther away Salvador Dalí becomes from me."

Ultimately, one could fill books with Dalí's crazy ideas. He wanted to do his painting with snail shells filled with paint, drive elephants over the Pyrenees, have his house guarded by rhinoceroses, and fill a Rolls-Royce with cauliflower. In 1964, Dalí closed himself into a plastic ball, in which he painted demons and angels while Parisian dancing girls stripped all around him. He had fish swimming around inside life-sized dolls, invented the "touchable film", and pronounced a baby to be the "vice-president of children". Dalí, who considered himself a monarchist and a Roman, said politics was history's dirty joke.

Of freedom:

"I'm against it. I'm for the Holy Inquisition, and this excess of freedom is ruining countries everywhere."

Of his contemporaries:

"Mao Tse-Tung is an extraordinary poet, in the manner of Homer. De Gaulle isn't authoritarian enough. Picasso is a genius, and so am I. Picasso is a billionaire, and so am I. Picasso is a communist, and I am not."

Of himself:

"I'm an exhibitionist. Life is too short to remain unnoticed. I am an average painter. If I were to compare myself with Vermeer or Velasquez, I would have to describe myself as a real artistic disaster. If I compare myself with my contemporaries, then I am simply the best."

Of money:

"It makes me happy that I earn 40,000 dollars by the time I sit down to breakfast."

Was Dalí an enigma? A provocateur? An enfant terrible?

In the foreword to Dalí's *Diary of a Genius*, Michel Déon writes:

"Dalí's most endearing features are his roots and his "antennae". Roots that reach deep down into the earth to explore everything that man has created in terms of delicacies (one of his favourite words), paintings, architecture, sculpture. Antennae that are directed toward the future, which they instantly sense, anticipate, and understand. It cannot be repeated often enough that Dalí is filled with insatiable intellectual curiosity. All achievements, all discoveries fall, defeated, in his works. And appear in them, in scarcely changed form."

[1] *Declaration of the Independence of the Imagination*, Salvador Dalí.
[2-5] *S. Dalí*, Karin von Maur, Hatje Verlag, 1989.

18

THE CONTRASTING SECRETS IN DALÍ'S WORK

Albert Field
Official Archivist for Salvador Dalí

THE DALÍ THEY SEE

There can be no question of the public recognition of Salvador Dalí. Ask the man in the street to name a modern artist, and he will likely name Dalí. There are several stages in this public awareness. He is well-known as a showman and as one of the great artists of the century. Those who are familiar with his popular works praise his technical skills and enjoy his wild imagination. It seems that everyone knows of the limp watches that appear in his paintings, though not everyone can give its title, *The Persistence of Memory*. Many viewers, drawn to his work by its bizarre content, come to appreciate both his technique and his imagery. They advance from incredulous shock to a vague and disturbed feeling that there is more than they can quite grasp. Something stirs in their psyches so that they feel, without knowing why, that they are in the presence of a genius. Some are surprised to find that they have become strangely fearful, but of what, they know not. A few find protection in laughter; others feel that Dalí has understood them, perhaps better than they understand themselves. This is how Dalí wanted it. He knew that every viewer would bring to his works a quantity of personal qualities that would cause him to see something different from the vision of all others and unique to his own personality. Each person assimilates into his own appreciation of a work that which corresponds most closely to his own peculiar perceptions and needs. Yet Dalí's art goes beyond understanding. For that is a far too rational process. He induces an unusual level of empathy between his work and the inner selves of the viewers.

THE KEY THEY MISS

Familiarity with Dalí's work reveals that amid the enormous diversity of his imagination there are a few images that appear again and again, more often in his earliest Surrealist paintings, but to some extent throughout his work. These fetish objects seem to have little in common: crutches, sea urchins, ants, lobsters, telephones and bread. That they must have been important to him is obvious, but what that importance is has eluded most observers.

Both the world of reality and the world of art are full of contrasts, and he used them as any artist would: to sharpen the message in the painting. The theme that is central to his thinking and to his work is the contrast between a hard outside and a soft inside. A prime example of this is the sea urchin: it has an exoskeleton (the shell is on its exterior), covered with spines that are very unpleasant to encounter. Within the shell is a soft body that is one Dalí's favourite foods. He has been known to eat a dozen at one meal. The sea urchin shell, shorn of spines, appears in several of his paintings.

Bread, too, is physically hard on the outside and soft within. When it is used in a communion service, its symbolic meaning reinforces the contrast. Dalí has said, it is *"one of the oldest themes of fetish obsessions in my life, the first, in fact, and the one to which I have most been faithful"*.

The difference between a madman and me is that I am not mad

The ant persists in his work throughout his life, hard on the outside and soft within. So do watches! A Dalínean watch is limp, not solid; it drapes itself over a branch. To us, a watch is the epitome of hardness, because both our expectation and our experience know only hard watches. When Dalí paints it, it has lost the quality as we know it. A practical watch tells time; a Dalí watch is timeless.

Many of his other fetishes echo the contrasts of hard and soft- the lobster, and of course, the telephone, which belong together. Dalí said, *"I do not understand why, when I ask for a grilled lobster in a restaurant, I am never served a cooked telephone..."*[1]. The lobster is easy to understand, but the telephone? Where is the softness? Look closely. Within the hard exterior is a softness surpassing that of all physical matter: the vibrations of electricity and of voice. This exterior/interior contrast is in accord with the psychological concept that people construct protective coverings (hard) over their vulnerable psyches (soft). Dalí was familiar with the work of Freud and his disciples, but his own iconography does not in any way derive from psychoanalytic thought.

THE "HARD" DALÍ

Dalí himself is hard and soft. What people see of him is his hard exterior. His showmanship, like the spines of the sea urchin, conceals a soft interior. His bizarre actions and extravagant statements serve two purposes: they attract the attention of the public, gain headlines and create a curiosity about his work. At the same time they deflect attention away from the real Dalí to the superficial exterior. Dalí's phenomenal technical skills are very visible in that part of his life which is the most external; his paintings that, when ready, leave him forever. These skills in line, composition, colour, and in the handling of his materials, produce permanent unchangeable "hardness". One cannot succeed as an artist, however much he may have the soul of one, unless he has the hands of one. If an aspiring painter cannot draw, there is no way he can express on canvas or paper his artistic ideas. Dalí's craftsmanship is superb. Whatever he draws, he draws well. And when he paints, his mastery of pigment and brush is such that the exquisite detail can be as photographic as of that of Vermeer, whom he greatly admired. Technical abilities are as necessary to the artist as the shell is to the lobster. Yet, they are only the hard exterior that contains a soft, living artist within.

THE "SOFT" DALÍ

Technical virtuosity makes an artisan competent, but it does not make an artist great. Imagination is deliriously fertile. An ordinary person is very careful to conceal whatever

If one understands one's painting in advance, one might as well not paint anything

aberrant thoughts or feelings may rise to the surface of his consciousness. Dalí, on the other hand, welcomes them and exposes then completely, without inhibition or concern for the mores of society.

A central principle of Surrealism was the evocation of surreal associations from the recesses of the subconscious. Yet, even when he was an active member of the Surrealist group in Paris, Dalí rejected their methodology. They favoured the establishment of contrived situations in order to stimulate subconscious inspiration. Dalí announced, to the considerable annoyance of several prominent members of the group, that he was able to suppress his reason at will and allow his "madness" free expression. Madness was a *sine qua non* of "genuine" Surrealism, and Dalí enthusiastically proclaimed that his madness was the most truly liberated.

He asserted, *"The difference between a madman and me is that I am not mad"*. He is not merely playing with words. Dalí's madness was real in the sense that ideas and images appeared to him in a greater quantity and intensity than they appear to "normal" people. This limitless source was the basis of his ability to create new images. The meaningful difference is that Dalí was "mad" and cultivated his "madness", while a madman does not know that he is mad, and his inability to grasp this fact is what establishes him as a mad. Dalí's paranoiac-critical method was the *"instantaneous and hand-drawn colour photograph of the superfine, extravagant, extraplastic, extra-pictorial, unexplored, super-pictorial, super-plastic, deceptive, hyper-normal, and sickly images of concrete irrationality"*[2].

The details of his painting were to be realistic, even photographic, but the composition was to be non-rational. Unlike some other surrealists, he did not merely rearrange elements in a work, he re-evaluated them in terms of their meaning to both the artist and the viewer. He accused rational thinking of being not only dull and uninspiring, but also unjust to the human spirit. It prevented the expression of man's true nature; while Dalí's work often caused the viewer to become aware of aspects of his own nature that were hidden (in fact, suppressed) and were inaccessible, except through the observation of uncontrolled imagery. Dalí gloried in his ability *"to systematise confusion"*[3].

THE SURREALIST OBJECT

'The surrealist object is one that is absolutely useless from a practical point of view, created wholly for the purpose of materialising in a fetishistic way, with the maximum of tangible reality, ideas and fantasies having a delirious character"[4] Salvador Dalí.

The official Surrealists, led by André Breton, frowned upon sculpture. They considered it a stale survival of the classical principles they scorned. In its place, they elevated the "object" to

a mystical level. Surrealist exhibitions of the 1930s abounded in *"objects"*, some of which were nothing more than haphazard assemblies of odds and ends, often with something consciously added to create a shocking effect. If there was any unifying principle among these items, it seems to have been only that anything so designated by an "artist" is art per se.

Dalí's *"Objet Surrealiste à Fonctionnement Symbolique"* (1932) included a sugar cube on a string suspended over a glass of milk in a shoe, together with a wooden spool and an erotic photograph. Its "function" was to shock, as was its alternate title *"The Pubic Hair of the Virgin."*

More serious was his *"Retrospective Tête de Femme"*, directly related to three of his fetishes: bread, ants and Millet's Angelus, in which he found a hidden eroticism not previously suspected.

'The surrealist object is impractical; it serves for nothing but to make men move, to exhaust them, to cretinize them. The surrealist object is made uniquely for the honour of the thought'[5] Salvador Dalí.

The famous soft watches
are nothing else than
the tender, extravagant, solitary,
paranoiac-critical Camembert
of time and space

THE FALSE THIRD DIMENSION

Even though Dalí remained primarily, and happily, a painter, he was dissatisfied with the two-dimensional flatness of canvas and paper which he felt arbitrarily limited his expression. As early as 1929, he painted a skyscape on a plaster form of human lips. His "New Amsterdam" (1974) is a trompe l'oeil painting on a bronze statue. In search of three-dimensionality he created bas-reliefs after the motifs of paintings. He experimented with holography, which fascinated him but offered inadequate scope for his artistic imagination. He painted several pairs of canvases that, when viewed stereoscopically (the canvases seen separately by each eye) produced the illusion of a human view of reality. He remained dissatisfied. Closer to his sculpture, are his plates in gold and silver and medals. His official medals for the 1984 Olympics use high relief to achieve an unusual feeling of action. But they are not yet three-dimensional! The same is true of his costume designs for ballets and theatre. The costumes contain unique additions such as crutches and strange protuberances so that the costumes, as well as the actors, appear in the third dimension. But they are not yet three-dimensional!

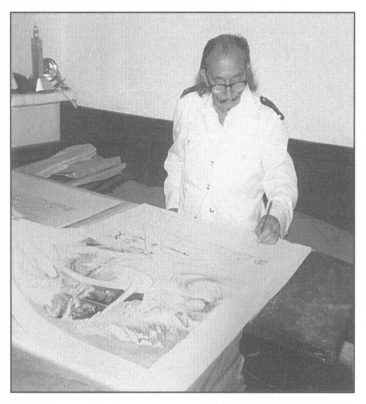

THE TRUE THIRD DIMENSION

Imitation and approximation of three-dimensionality still remained unsatisfactory for Dalí. Nothing can take the place of a sculpture, which the viewer can see, with varied effect, from multiple perspectives.

Dalí's interest in mere objects, whether haphazardly assembled or designed by the subconscious, diminished as he saw how empty such objects could be. Sculpture brought a new dimension to his work, not only in the mathematical or geometric sense of the word.

Dalí's description of his paranoiac-critical method defines his intentions: *"My whole ambition is to materialise the image of concrete irrationality with the most imperialistic fury of precision in order that the world of imagination and concrete irrationality may be as objectively evident, of the same consistency, of the same durability, of the same persuasive, cognoscitive and communicative thickness as that of the exterior world of phenomenal reality"*. Each medium imposes its own limitations. The sculptor must forego the use of colour and must rely on form and texture instead. Dalí's feeling for form was both scientific and metaphysical:

"We know today that form is always the product of an inquisitorial process of matter. The specific reaction of matter when subjected to the terrible coercion of space choking it on all sides, pressing and squeezing it out, producing the swellings that burst from its life to the exact limits of the rigorous contours of its own originality of reaction. How many times matter endowed with a too-absolute impulse is annihilated; whereas another bit of matter, which tries to do only what it can and is better adapted to the pleasure of moulding itself by contracting in its own way before the tyrannical impact of space, is able to invent its own original form of life."[6]

He went on to observe:

"It is not known, through recent findings in morphology (glory be to Goethe for having invented this word that would have appealed to Leonardo), that most often it is precisely the heterogeneous and anarchistic tendencies offering the greatest complexity of antagonisms that lead to the triumphant reign of the most rigorous hierarchies of form"[7].

Dalí the sculptor begins with a soft mass of wax or clay. He imposes on it his form, making concrete the irrationality of his imagination. When he has finished pressing and squeezing out the pliant matter that initially was an amorphous nothing, he casts it in bronze so that it can take place in the exterior world, thereby changing his creation from soft to hard. Throughout his work, his fetishes and obsessions continue to appear insofar as they can be translated into solid matter. The limp watch can be the dominant element in one piece (*The Persistence of Memory*) and a subtle clue in the composition of another (*Space Venus*). The ant crawls on the smooth surface of Venus (*Space Venus*). The crutch supports in a variety of ways. It may be the sole foundation for a figure (*Venus with Head of Roses*) or the necessary support of a Dalinian extension that is incapable of self-support (*Atavistic Vestiges After the Rain*).

Sculpture is not merely hard on the outside - it freezes whatever softness may have been within and preserves its essence and its significant aspect of Dalí's artistic reaction; they provide a summary of his focus on form. They are, in fact, Surrealism in the third dimension.

[1] *The Secret Life of Salvador Dalí.*
[2] *Conquest of the Irrational.*
[3] *La Femme Visible.*
[4] *Surréalisme au Service de la Révolution.*
[5] *Honneur à l'Objet.*

[6] Quoted by J.T.Soby in the 1941 catalogue of the Salvador Dalí exhibition at the New York Museum of Modern Art.
[7] *Dalí: a Study of His Art in Jewels.*

Dreams & Fantasy

Sensuality & Femininity

Religion & Mythology

Dream

Throughout his lifetime, Dalí was greatly preoccupied by the accurate portrayal of the true content of his inner mind through his artwork, claiming that only through art was he able to give free rein to the unconscious, and thus bypass the filter of human attempts at rationality. He was fascinated by the world of dreams and fantasy. It seems that the contrast, and often the conflict, between dreams and reality is what led Dalí to embrace Surrealism. He believed that dreams were the only true, accurate, and meaningful expression of his personality. An avid follower of Freud, like many others within the Surrealist movement, Dalí's interest in dreams, their meanings and their relationship to complete 'freedom' led him to align himself strongly with the beliefs expounded by Freud in his *Interpretation of Dreams*. Dalí readily welcomed the opportunity to meet with Freud in London in the late 1930s, and this meeting served to further increase his admiration of the great psychoanalyst. The respect was reciprocated, as can be noted in Freud's letter to Stefan Zweig after their meeting:

"I really owe you thanks for bringing yesterday's visitor. For until now, I have been inclined to regard the Surrealists, who have apparently adopted me as their patron saint, as complete fools (let us say 95%, as with alcohol): That young Spaniard, with his candid, fanatical eyes and his undeniable technical mastery has changed my estimate."

& Fantasy

Many of Dalí's most important works were the result of the wild images that came to him in dreams, in combination with the violent feelings that surfaced in opposition to the ordinary world, the world of 'reason'. His earlier works focused particularly on many of these dream images. By making himself 'the other', Dalí was able to explore himself, his dreams and his thoughts, albeit not impartially. One of the striking differences between Dalí and many of the artists within the Surrealist movement was Dalí's construction of his paranoiac-critical method. This method of rereading objects or situations was developed by Dalí in order to 'discover' the hidden meanings that are always present. Dalí's method involved organisation of the symbols presented to the self by the unconscious in such a way that the artist is then able to take advantage and utilise what the unconscious is trying to relate.

The melted clocks for which Dalí is most famous, seen in the sculptures *Persistence of Memory* and *Profile of Time* depict Dalí's fantastical relationship with time, his perception of its constricting limitations and the importance he believed to be inherent in memory. Dalí's feelings about the clock, the keeper of time, are evident as he most often portrays the clock as soft, a type of symbolism he reserved only for objects that he reviled. In *La Vie Secrete*, Dalí's autobiography published in 1942, the artist stated, *"The mechanical object was to become my worst enemy, and as for watches, they would have to be soft, or not be at all!"*. Humans cannot rely on the non-dreaming world as a true one. This theme is repeated yet again in his sculpture of the *Horse Saddled with Time*. In this sculpture, time, a representation of the world of the waking and the world of repression, is riding a horse, this animal in turn representing life. Dalí has embodied society's restrictions in this sculpture, showing the unconscious, which is the true psyche of the individual, is constantly trying to reveal itself.

Through illustration of great themes of literature, Dalí continued his exploration of the symbolism of pure fantasy and dreams while remaining awake. He was drawn to *Alice in Wonderland*, clearly dear to him both in terms of characters and for its story line. Alice returns from her adventure in Wonderland unscathed, her childlike innocence and her unanswerable logic preserved. Through illustrating other books, Dalí continued his escape to pure fantasy, demonstrating yet again his preference for a dreaming state. The graphic series *La Vida es Sueño* (Life is a Dream), is another prime example, specifically referring to a life lived through dreams and a distorted, more amusing (more real?) option to reality.

Dalí's fantasy was not limited solely to the psychological deconstruction of the world in which he lived. He was also enthralled with the world as it would be in the future, the possibilities and flexibility that could change the world. The graphics illustrating the books *Aprés 50 Ans de Surrealisme*, *Dix Recettes d'Immortalité*, and *Alchimie des Philosophes* all clearly illustrate the time he devoted toward futuristic fantasy. *Dix Recettes d'Immortalité* is a collection of graphics contained in a box deigned by Dalí, accessorised with a telephone handle and two fried egg locks. The vivid colours and abstract designs in *Alchimie des Philosophes* bring to mind an alternative chaotic version of life, while in the graphics of *Aprés 50 Ans de Surrealisme*, Dalí creates his own interpretation of a possible future.

As a way to know himself better, Dalí attempted to reconstruct his surroundings. He experimented with the creation of startlingly unusual furniture, like the *Leda low table* and the *Cajones lamp*. The Daum glass sculptures, with their airy quality and their vivid colours, and Dalí's gold objects, are a clear link to a more fantastical world. Not only was Dalí modifying objects, such as gold to coins to figures, he was in turn modifying the world around him.

*The human body…
is full of
secret drawers that
can only be opened
by psychoanalysis*

Alice in Wonderland
1977-84
BRONZE
227 X 46 X 111 CM

**The Horse Saddled
with Time**
1980
BRONZE
95 X 186 CM

Space Elephant
1980
BRONZE
227 X 58 X 150 CM

*What is important
is to spread confusion,
not to eliminate it*

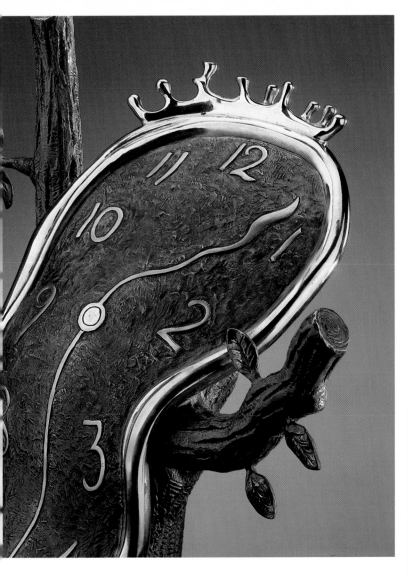

Nobility of Time
1977-84
BRONZE
154 X 89 X 70 CM

Persistence of Memory
1980
BRONZE
191 X 90 X 40 CM

Profile of Time
1972
BRONZE
150 X 100 X 60 CM

Femme Giraffe
1973
BRONZE
240 X 35.5 X 120 CM

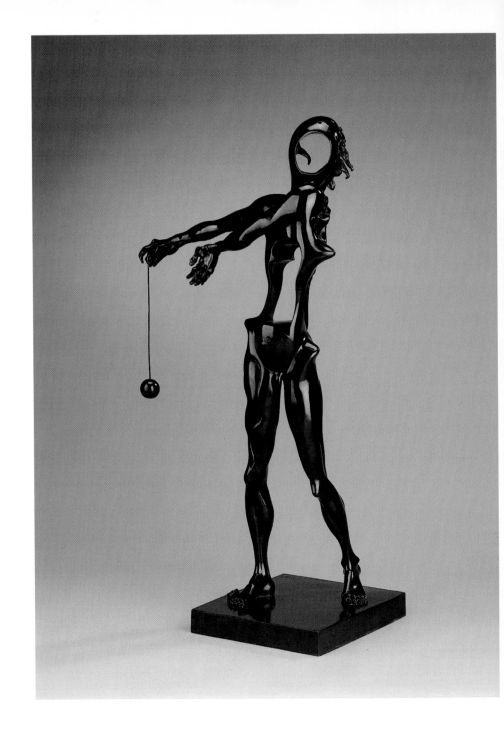

Homage to Newton
1969
BRONZE
132 X 120 X 50 CM

Golden Newton
1968
BRONZE
25.4 CM

Newton without Arms
1968
BRONZE
9 X 27 X 9 CM

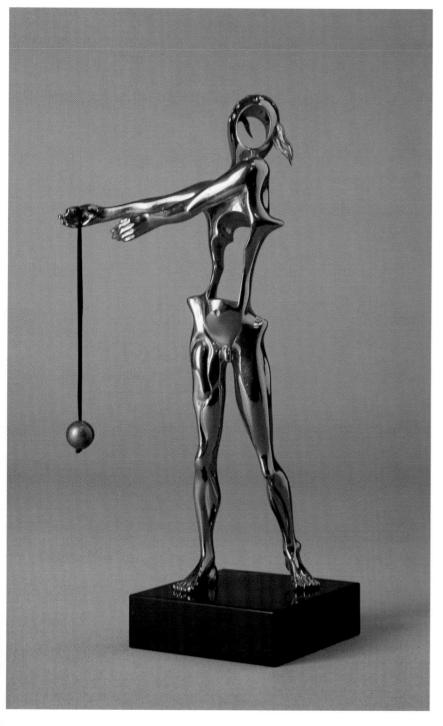

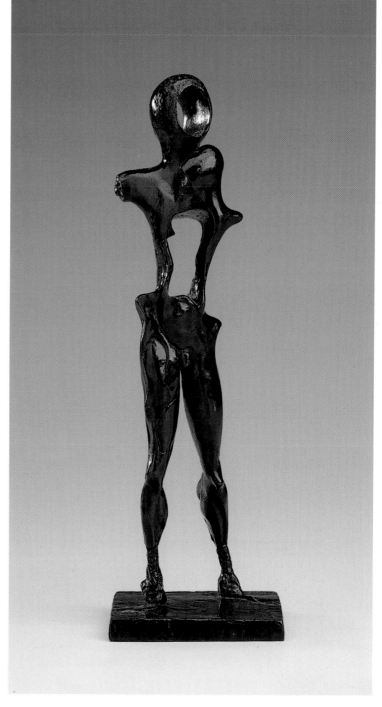

*I do not believe that reality
can be everywhere at the same time
whereas God can be*

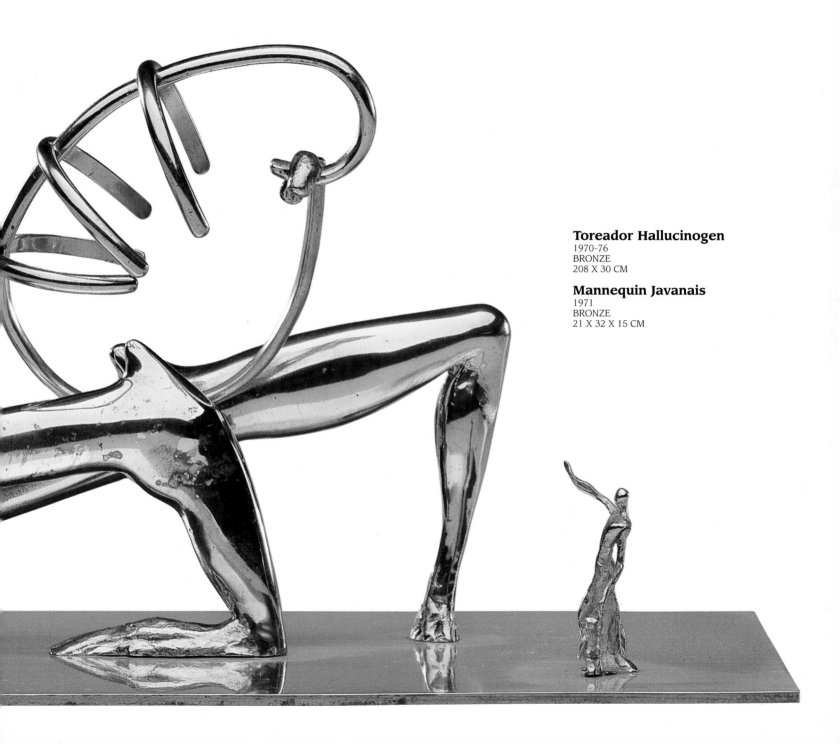

Toreador Hallucinogen
1970-76
BRONZE
208 X 30 CM

Mannequin Javanais
1971
BRONZE
21 X 32 X 15 CM

**Les Vestiges Ataviques
après la Pluie**
1969
BRONZE
28 X 20 X 34 CM

**La Chaise
aux Cuillères**
1960-74
BRONZE
111 X 36 X 46 CM

**La Masque Funéraire
de Napoléon**
1970
BRONZE
22 X 19 X 28 CM

Le Cygne-Elephant
1967
BRONZE
13 X 20 X 10 CM

Pieuvre
1970
MIXED MEDIA
50 X 31 X 10 CM

Caduceus
1985
MIXED MEDIA
14 X 26 CM; 14 X 29 CM

Esclave de Michelin
1966
BRONZE
30 X 18 X 18 CM

*The fact that I myself
do not understand
the meaning of my paintings
at the time that I am painting them
does not mean
that they have no meaning*

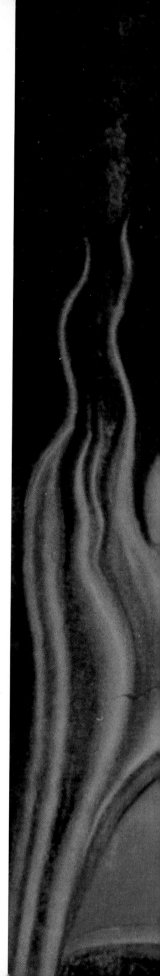

Spellbound
1945
OIL ON CANVAS,
TWO PARTS EACH,
5.2 X 5.75 M

The students considered me
a reactionary, an enemy
of progress and of liberty.
They called themselves revolutionaries
and innovators, because all
of a sudden they were allowed to paint
as they pleased.
How stupid people can be!

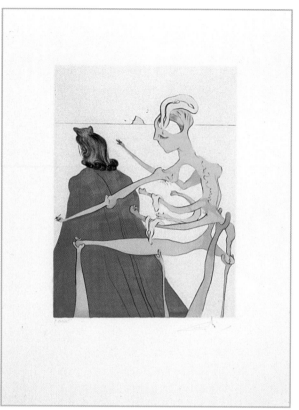

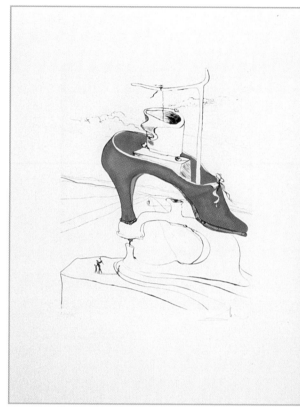

**Après 50 Ans
de Surrealisme**
1974
BRONZE
12 DRYPOINT ETCHINGS
WATERCOLOURED BY HAND
50 X 65 CM

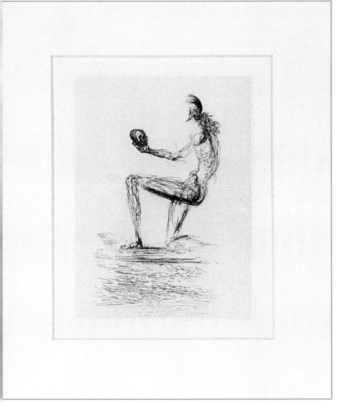

**Chants
de Maldoror**
1934
30 DRYPOINT,
ENGRAVINGS
30 X 19 CM

Don Quichotte
1957
12 LITHOGRAPHS, WATERCOLOUR
AND COLLAGE
41 X 33 CM

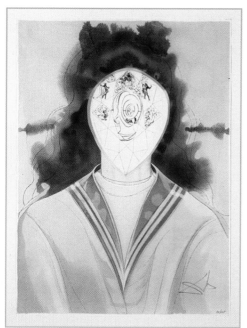

Alchimie des Philosophes
1976
10 LITHOGRAPHS, SERIGRAPHS
76 X 56 CM

Is it hard to love Dalí?
No, it's soft

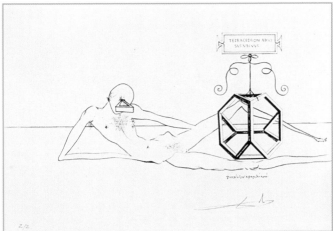

Dix Recettes d'Immortalité
1973
14 MULTI-MEDIA
43 X 61 CM

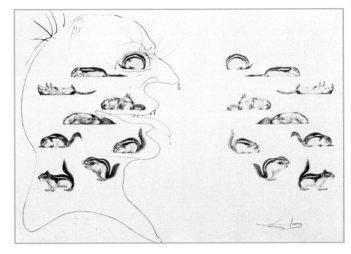

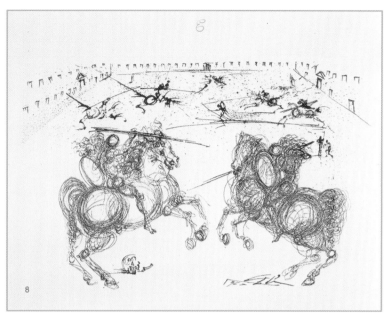

La Vida es Sueno
1975
17 COLOURED ETCHINGS
40 X 30 CM

Caprices de Goya
1977
59 DRYPOINTS ETCHINGS
39 X 31 CM

**Caprices de Goya
interpreted by Dalí**
1977
59 DRYPOINTS ETCHINGS
39 X 31 CM

*There is less madness
to my method
than there is method
to my madness*

Fran.co Goya y Lucientes, Pintor

Unos à otros

Ia es hora.

Torcuato de Tarso

Pirueta de plátano

Leda low table
1937-85
VARIOUS MATERIALS
190 X 45 X 42 CM

Bracelli lamp
1937-85
VARIOUS MATERIALS
37 X 28 X 180 CM

Leda armchair
1937-85
VARIOUS MATERIALS
60 X 50 X 90 CM

Cajones lamp
1937-85
VARIOUS MATERIALS
30 X 30 X 67 CM

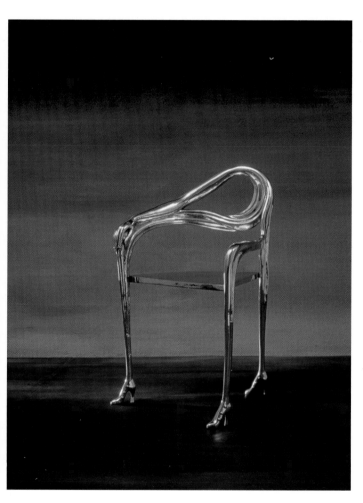

Ideas are made to be copied.
I have enough ideas to sell them on.
I prefer that they are stolen so that I don't have
to actually use them myself

Mirror
1967
GOLD

Isis - Portrait Frame
1967
GOLD

*The least
one can ask
of a sculpture
is that it does not
move*

*Life is aspiration,
respiration
and expiration*

Dali Flower
1967
GOLD

Glorious Sun
1967
GOLD

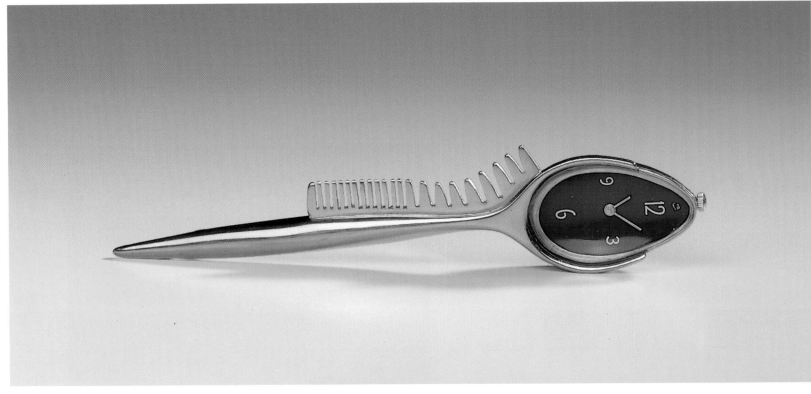

Montre Petit Cuillère
1959
GOLD
11.3 CM

**Mafalda Davis
Tableware**
1957
VERMEILLE
AND SEMI-PRECIOUS STONES
11.9 X 23.8 CM

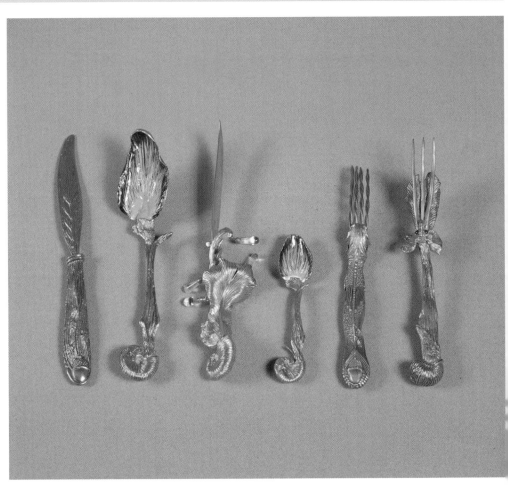

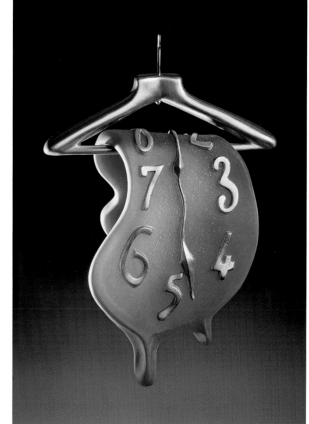

Le Désir Hyperrationnel
1984
PÂTE DE VERRE
42 X 25 CM

Débris d'une automobile
1984
PÂTE DE VERRE
42 X 25 CM

Montre Molle
1984
PÂTE DE VERRE
42 X 25 CM

Vénus de Milo Hystérique
1984
PÂTE DE VERRE
42 X 25 CM

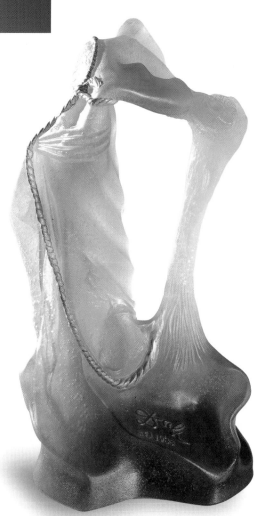

Sensuality

It is impossible to fully separate any artist's lifelong themes. Dalí's artworks which focus on sensuality and femininity are often recurring images that he stumbled upon in his dreams. Freud identifies the unconscious as being composed of true repressed sexual desire and sexual drive. Repeatedly, Dalí created works detailing his obsession with sexual anxieties in relation to his sexual identity. Throughout his youth Dalí was plagued by the trait of severe insecurity and fear in relation to women and sexual relations. However, Dalí's relationship with Gala played a major part in changing his idea towards femininity and the female form.

Dalí's depiction of the female form was influenced most strongly by Gala, his wife and inspirational creative muse. Dalí was captivated by this passionate Russian whom he met in 1929, and whom he regarded as the ideal representation of womanhood. Gala was already married to the established poet Paul Eluard, but left him for Dalí soon after their initial encounter. During this period Dalí suffered from fits of hysterical laughter. He credited Gala with curing him, both from these fits, as well as from his own sexual anxieties. The two remained inseparable until her death in 1982. Dalí clearly integrated Gala's ideal form into most of his artwork, stating in *La Vie Secrete* that he in fact recognised Gala from the back before he knew her. In retrospect, he had been waiting for her.

Femininity

However, throughout his life it is evident that he remained interested in experimentation both with accepted notions of sensuality as well as with studies of the radically unusual.

The topic of Sensuality & Femininity is strongly represented by several famous and important pieces. Of particular interest is the renowned *Mae West Lips Sofa*, originally created by Dalí in the late 1930s and based on the voluptuous actress known for her provocative one-liners. Another famous piece is the *Buste de Femme Retrospectif* sculpture, which remains one of the defining classics of Surrealism from the 1930s. The latter includes several Dalínean recurring images, such as ants, bread, and an adaptation of Millet's *Angelus.* Dalí was obsessed with this painting, and integrated it into many of his pieces. Ants are Dalí's representation of anxiety, nervousness and decay, while food symbolises sexual desire. Dalí's adoration of bread, hard on the outside and soft on the inside, like so many of his other fetishes, endured as an obsession throughout his entire life.

Woman Aflame is representative of two other symbols which frequently permeate Dalí's work. The first is the crutch. Dalí, in *La Vie Secrete*, stated that upon the discovery of a crutch, the item "*communicated to me an assurance, an arrogance*

even, which I had never been capable of until then." (p. 90). He also calls it
"the symbol of death" and *"the symbol of resurrection"*. In Dalí's artworks the crutch
often symbolises a blend of authority, stability, and (often sexual) power.
The second symbol found in *Woman Aflame*, like *Venus Traversèe par les Longs Tiroirs*, is the presence of drawers. Dalí once explained the drawers in his figures
as a Freudian outgrowth of the natural curiosity of children to investigate
enclosed spaces in order to satisfy both the desire to know what is there,
and the desire to exorcise the fear that the unknown may do harm.
Freud explained that drawers represent the concealed sexuality of woman.
In these two sculptures, Dalí shows many of the drawers open, indicating
that their secrets are known and no longer to be feared.

Several examples of Dalí's famous portfolios of graphics illustrating major themes of literature are included in this area. Among the graphics on display are the 10 rare lithographs from the series *Romeo and Juliet*, the 14 erotic *Casanova* images, the 10 etchings of the series *Le Décaméron*, and the 15 engravings from the *L'Art d'Aimer*. The latter were based on Ovid's classic, found to be so scandalous by Roman society of the day that it led to Ovid's permanent exile to the Black Sea. Dalí's portrayal of women was almost always highly erotic, and generally linked with his ideals of authority. In *La Vie Secrete*, the artist stated, *"It seemed to me so natural that all women should rush out into the street every afternoon with their brain tormented by the same idea, by the same erotic fantasies as mine. But no!"* (p. 216) By delving into the sexuality of the characters in literature, Dalí was also experimenting and coming to terms with his own sexual nature.

**Le Cabinet
Anthropomorphique**
1982
BRONZE
96 X 180 X 60 CM

*Intelligent artists are those
who are capable of expressing
the most wild and chaotic experiments
into classical form.
I have done all kinds of experiments.
I have even painted with a gun!*

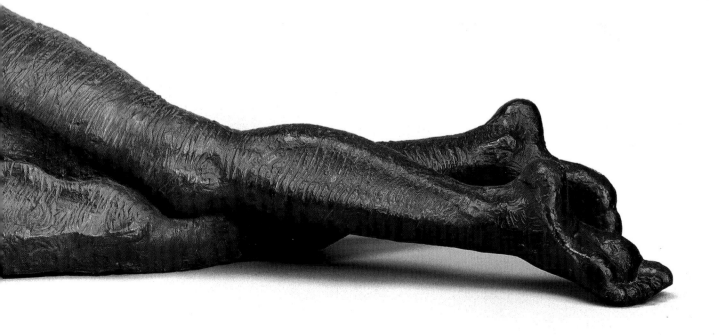

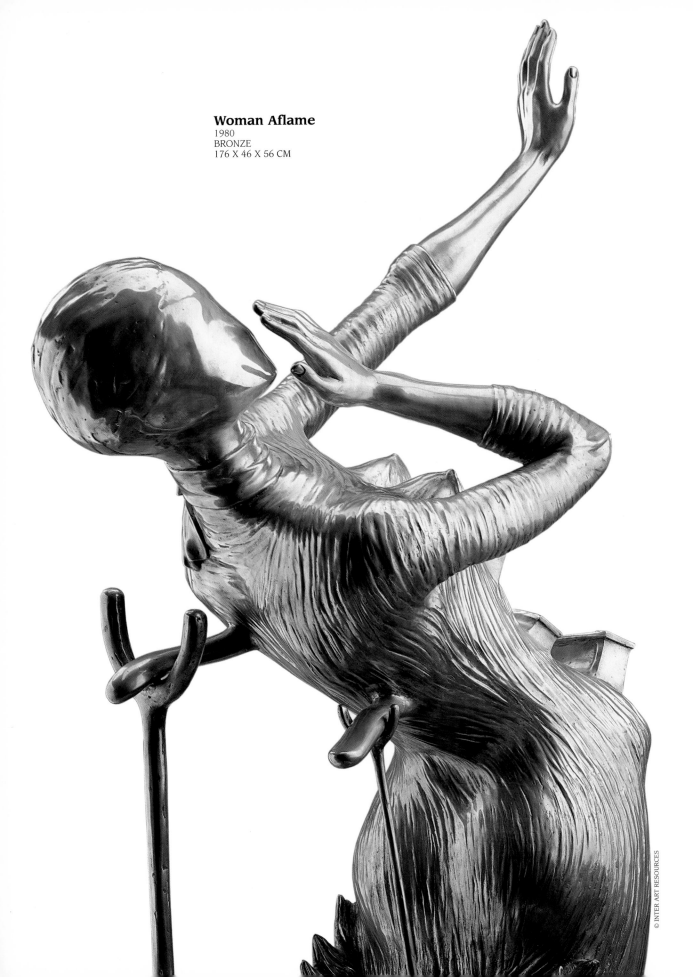

Woman Aflame
1980
BRONZE
176 X 46 X 56 CM

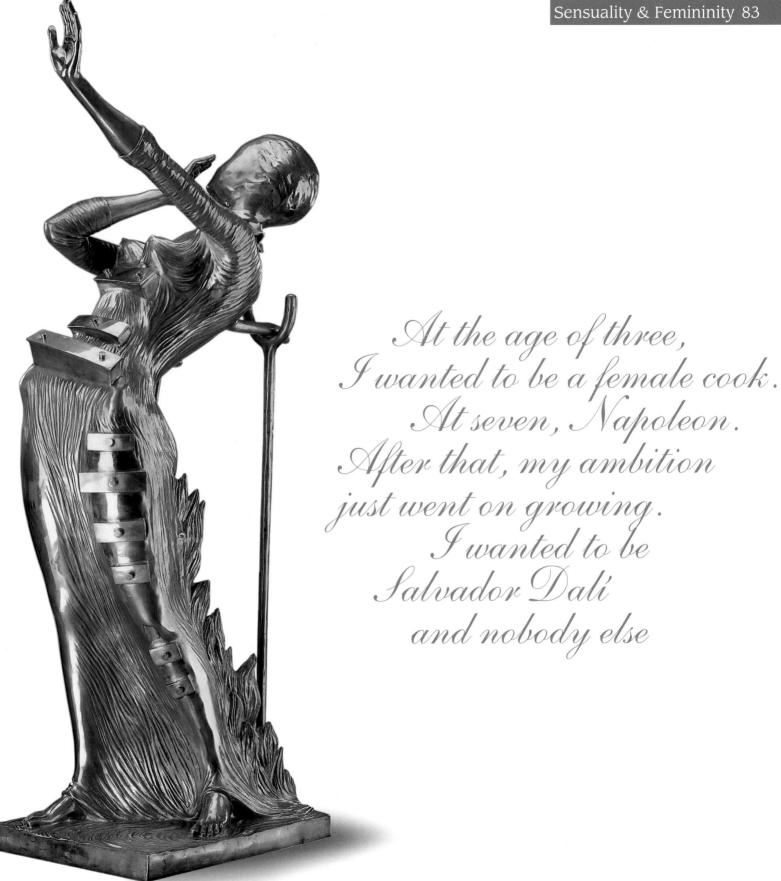

*At the age of three,
I wanted to be a female cook.
At seven, Napoleon.
After that, my ambition
just went on growing.
I wanted to be
Salvador Dalí
and nobody else*

Homage to Terpsichore
1977-84
BRONZE
187 X 103 X 55 CM

Space Venus
1977-84
BRONZE
124 X 61 X 62 CM

*Take me,
I am the drug.
Take me,
I am the
hallucinogenic*

Mae West Lips Sofa
1936-95
VARIOUS MATERIALS
224 X 75 X 85 CM

**Objet Surréaliste
à Fonctionnement
Symbolique**
1932-75
VARIOUS MATERIALS
52 X 34 X 23 CM

Papillon et la Flamme
1972
BRONZE
60 X 11 X 9 CM

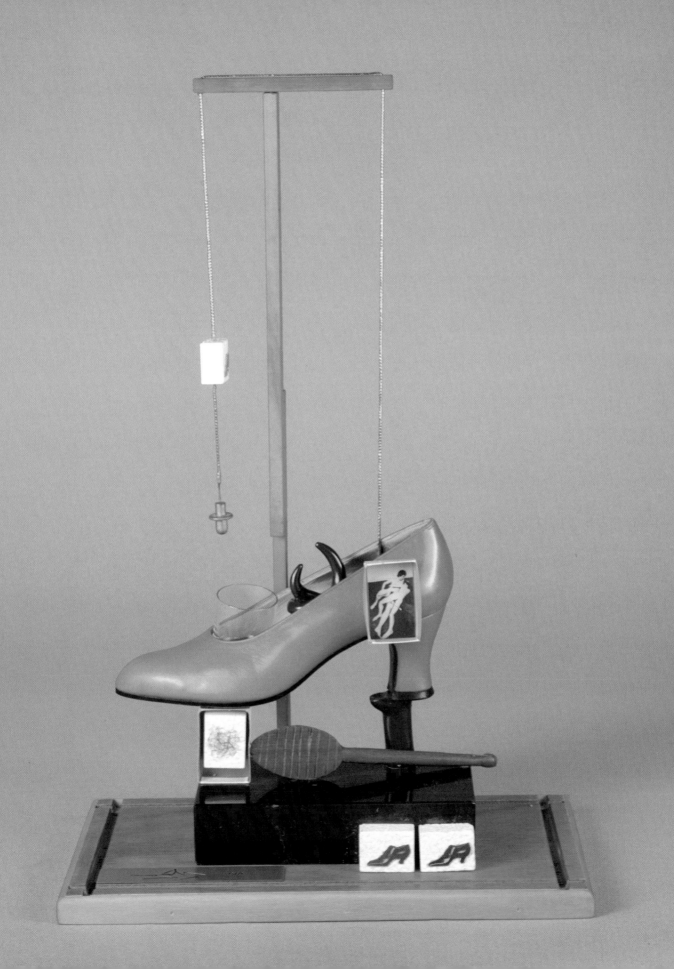

**Nu Féminin Hystérique
et Aérodynamique**
1934-73
BRONZE
46 X 26 X 15 CM

La Premonition des Tiroirs
1973
BRONZE
21 X 39 X 28 CM

*I cannot understand why
people are so incapable of fantasy
that bus drivers don't from time to time
break the windows at a department store
to pick up some gifts for their family*

**Buste de Femme
Retrospectif**
1933-70
BRONZE
54 X 35 X 10 CM

*The one thing
of which
the world
will never
have enough
is exaggeration*

**Venus Traversèe
par les Longs Tiroirs**
1988
BRONZE
218 X 82.5 X 82 CM

The envy
of other artists
has always been
the barometer
of my success

Le Cendrier
1959
BRONZE
55 CM

La Tasse pour ne pas Boire
1965
GOLD-PLATED BRONZE
10 X 14 X 15 CM

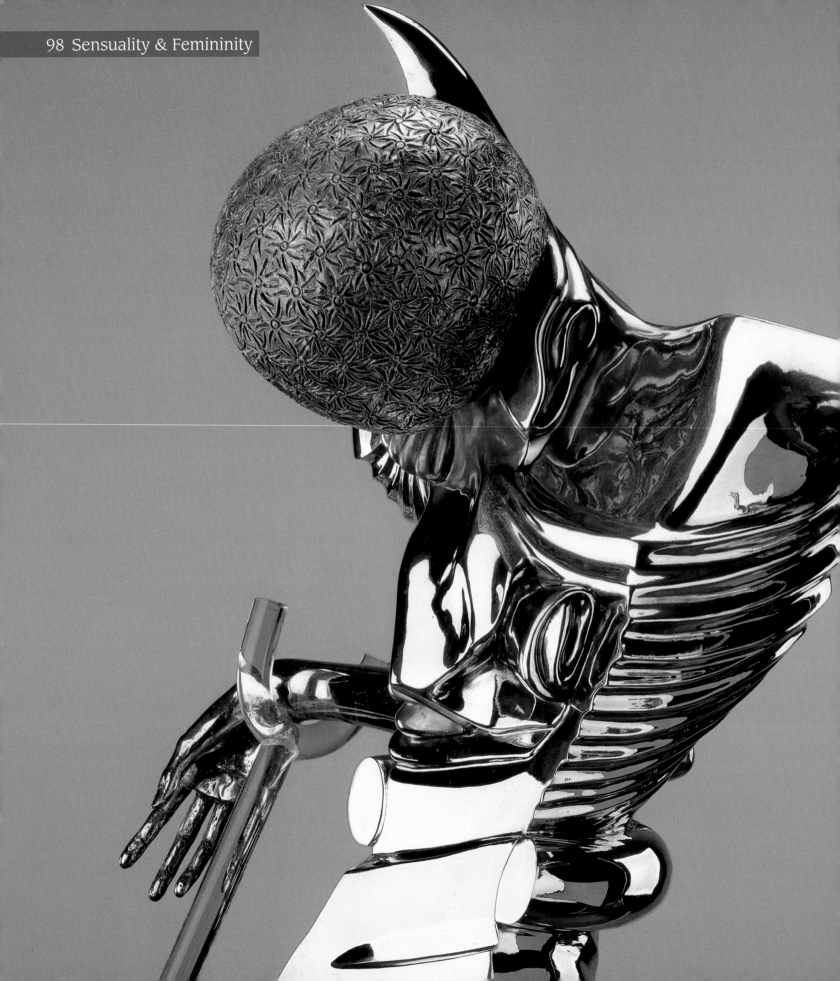

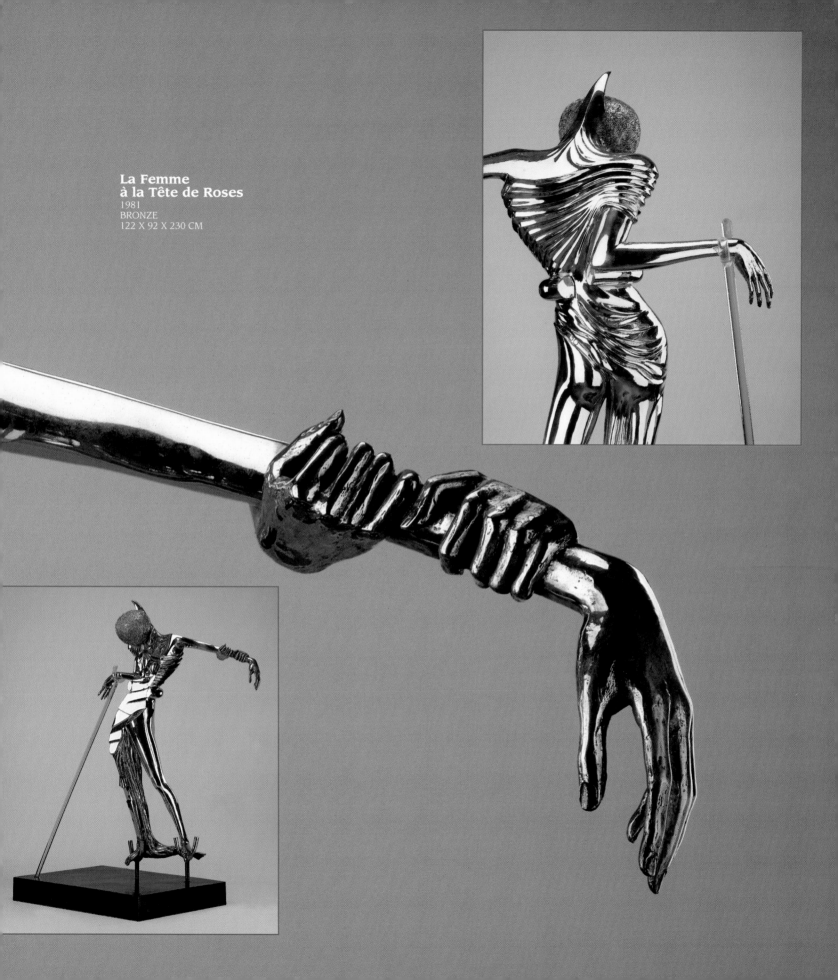

**La Femme
à la Tête de Roses**
1981
BRONZE
122 X 92 X 230 CM

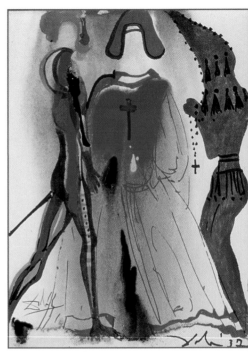

Romeo and Juliet
1967
10 LITHOGRAPHS
52 X 42 CM

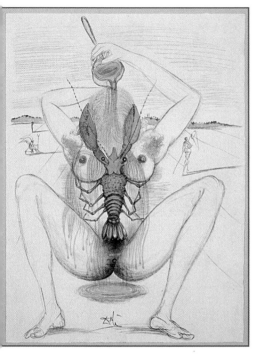

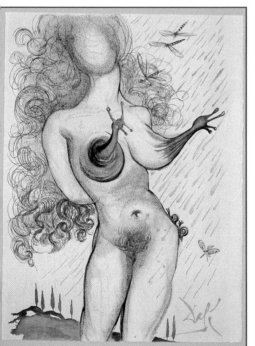

Casanova
1967
14 LITHOGRAPHS
28 X 38 CM

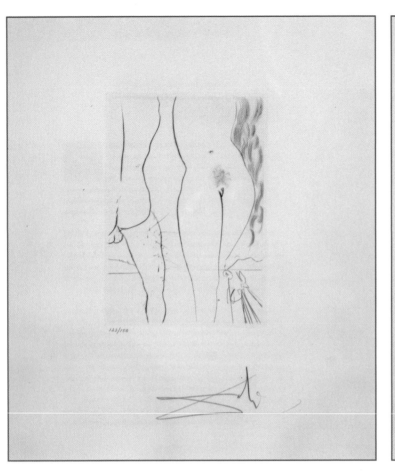

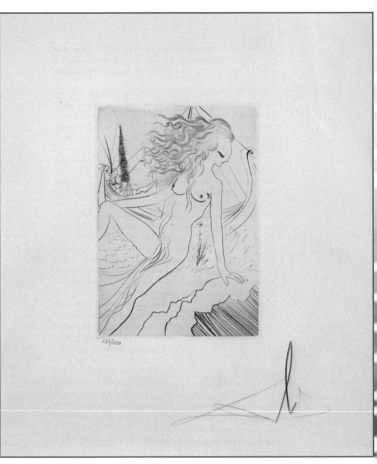

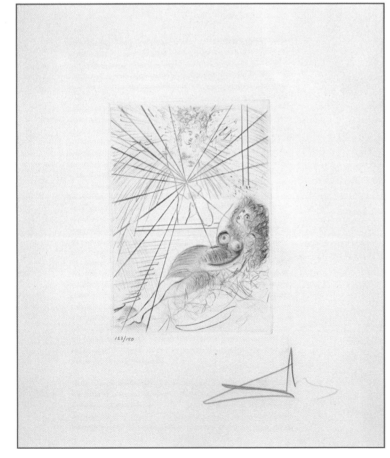

Décaméron
1972
10 DRYPOINTS ETCHINGS
45 X 32 CM

L'Art d'Aimer
1978
15 WOOD ENGRAVINGS
AND COLOURED LITHOGRAPHS
56 X 38 CM

Les Amours Jaunes
1974
9 ETCHINGS
30 X 21 CM

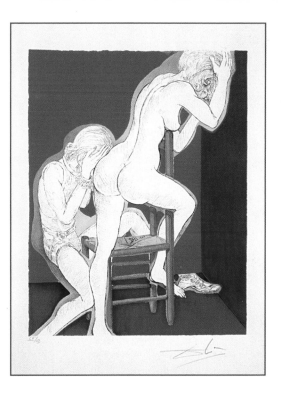

Le Marquis de Sade
1968
25 LITHOGRAPHS
50 X 40 CM

Tarot
1970
COLLAGE WITH WATERCOLOUR
50 X 32 CM

*Beauty
will either be edible,
or will not be*

I'm in a permanent state
of intellectual erection

Tarot
1970
COLLAGE WITH WATERCOLOUR
50 X 32 CM

SALVADOR DALI

Les
métamorphoses
érotiques

Choix de dessins exécutés de 1940 à 1968

A L'Érotitiade

121/150

Metamorphoses Erotiques
1969
11 DRYPOINTS AND ILLUSTRATIONS
26 X 32 CM

AGAINST:	FOR:
simplicity	*complexity*
uniformity	*diversity*
equality	*hierarchy*
the collective	*the individual*
politics	*metaphysics*
music	*architecture*
nature	*beauty*
progress	*eternity*
mechanics	*dreams*
the abstract	*the concrete*
youth	*maturity*
opportunism	*fanaticism*
spinach	*snails*
cinema	*theatre*
the sun	*the moon*
revolution	*tradition*
Michelangelo	*Raphael*
Rembrandt	*Vermeer*
the wild	*civilisation*
philosophy	*religion*
medicine	*magic*
mountains	*the seaside*
phantoms	*spectres*
women	*Gala*
men	*myself*
Time	*melted watches*
skepticism	*folly*

Religion & Myth

Dalí had a tempestuous relationship with the Catholic Church throughout his life. Like other intellectuals and artists of the time, Dalí attempted to reject his faith, along with many other bourgeois traditions, in the 1920s and 1930s. His actions were part of his determination to live a life out of the ordinary, a life in which he would not compromise by accepting banal tradition, and instead, was resolved to ceaselessly question everything. The Surrealist movement was strongly linked with mythology during this period, holding the general belief that the individual psyche was reflected in the myths of a society, and vice versa. The idea that myths dealt with important and often repressed aspects of human nature obviously had a great influence on Dalí as well, as he was completely devoted to his own self-analysis.

Dalí read philosophy extensively, and his father's atheism also led him to question his own religious views. His mother instead was a devout Catholic, and, after much exploration, Dalí never fully succeeded in abandoning the faith of his childhood. During the 1920s and 1930s, some of his paintings were considered profane. His pieces containing reference to masturbation were particularly shocking at the time, and considered to be a sin. The artist's works over his many years of creation show clearly that he delved deeply into studies and explorations of various types of religion, particularly after his official break with the Surrealist movement in the 1940s. Throughout the late 1940s and 1950s Dalí was enthralled with molecular biology and nuclear physics, often entwining these ideas with those of religion. For example, he dreamt that he saw an atom which became Christ – the centre of the universe. Dalí remained intrigued by the melodrama of religious imagery throughout his lifetime.

One of Dalí's most important sculptures, *St. George and the Dragon*, a Surrealistic interpretation of a defining Christian story, was presented to Pope John Paul II by the Stratton Foundation for display in the Vatican's permanent collection.

Among the sculptural works featured is *Yang et Yin*, Dalí's interpretation of the Eastern ideology of balance in nature. Also present is *The Vision of the Angel*, which is a clear example of Dalí's interest in the flexibility of theological compositions. God is represented by a large thumb, from which all life emerges (represented by branches), and is flanked on both sides by a man (vitality) and an angel (meditative spirit). *The Snail and the Angel* is a sculpture incorporating two of Dalí's favourite images, ever-recurring in his work. Dalí again uses sharp contrasts (the slow movement of the snail contrasted with the speed of the small winged messenger) to further accentuate the attributes, or characteristics, of each figure. Both religion and mythology constantly permeate his work.

Two of Dalí's most famous masterpieces are included in this area, the illustrations of *The Bible*, and of Dante's spectacular *Divine Comedy*. Both epic works include over 100 graphics, and each is a prime example of Dalí's vivid imagination and his capability to reinterpret classic works using as his only medium his own unique and bizarre vision. The time he devoted to the perfection of these graphic masterpieces closely correlated with his ongoing spiritual development. His interest in the Judeo-Christian tradition continued as he illustrated the classics *Aliyah, Le Douze Tribus d'Israel,* and *Song of Songs of Solomon.* The broad range of methods he used for these texts show how they permeated his life – from the simplistic, bright coloured *Le Douze Tribus d'Israel*, to the more intense, dark coloured *Aliyah*. Religion was an expression for his every mood.

The interlacing of the above three groups continues in the primarily religious images of *Eve and the Serpent* and the *Coronation de San Salvador d'Orta*. The former links Dalí's ideas of femininity and eroticism with the religion that so permeated his life. The latter obviously had personal connotations for Dalí himself, as so often with Dalí, he saw himself everywhere:

"My whole life has been determined by those two antagonistic ideas, the top and the bottom. Since my earliest childhood I have desperately striven to be at the 'top'. I have reached it, and now that I am there I shall remain there until I die." (*La Vie Secrete*, p. 72)

**St. George
and the Dragon**
1977-84
BRONZE
148 X 138 X 84 CM

**The Vision
of the Angel**
1977-84
BRONZE
140 X 98 X 99 CM

The Snail and the Angel
1977-84
BRONZE
151 X 183 X 108 CM

*Every morning upon awakening,
I experience a supreme pleasure:
that of being Salvador Dalí...
And I ask myself, wonderstruck,
what prodigious thing will he do today,
this Salvador Dalí*

*Modesty
is not exactly
my speciality*

The Unicorn
1977-84
BRONZE
183 X 165 X 113 CM

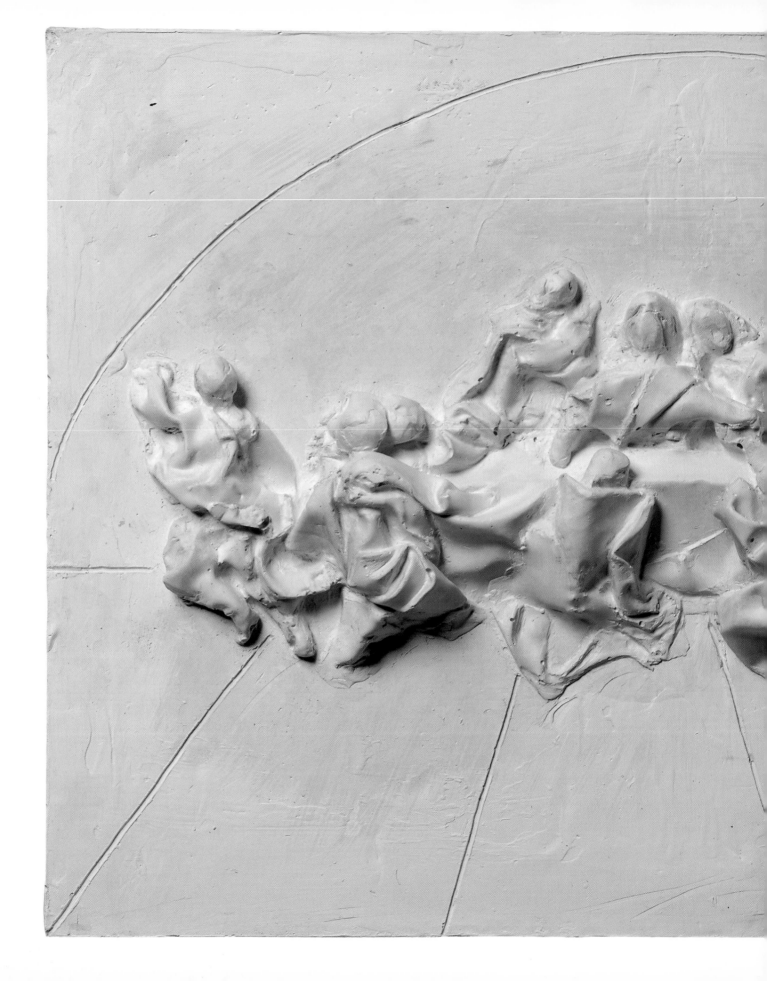

The Last Supper
1978
TERRACOTTA
45.5 X 61 X 6 CM

Art is a weapon of war
engaged by desire
in its battle for supremacy
against the principles of reality

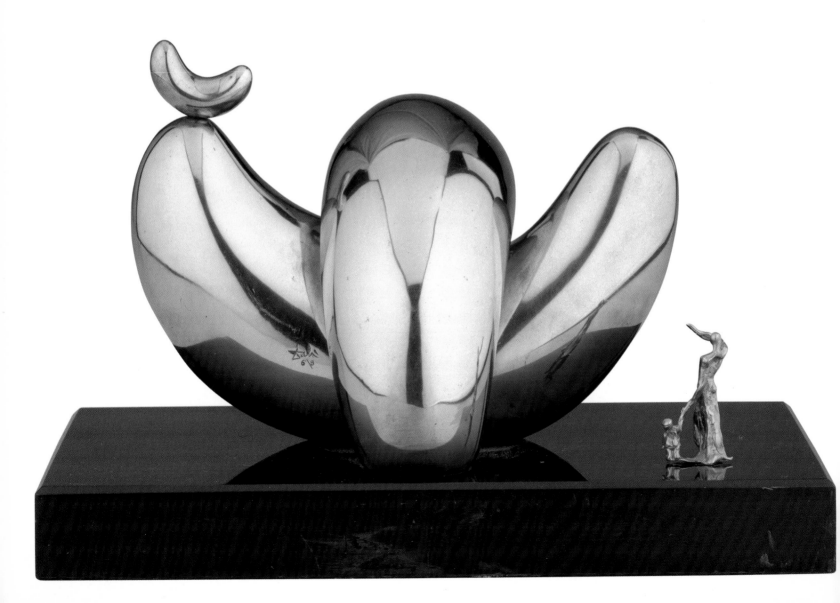

Yang et Yin
1973
BRONZE
32 X 20 X 25 CM

Christ Cubique
1964
BRONZE
55 X 24.5 X 22

Christ on the Cross
1970 C.
BRONZE
20 X 20 X 60 CM

The Minotaur
1988
BRONZE

*I love my enemies
when they are intelligent
as much as I hate
those who are stupid
when they are
defending me*

The Birdman
1968
BRONZE
83 X 20 X 25 CM

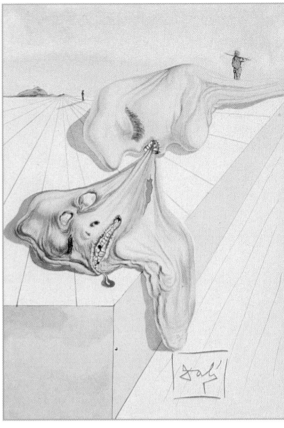

Divine Comedy

1960
103 COLOURED
WOOD ENGRAVINGS
33 X 26 CM

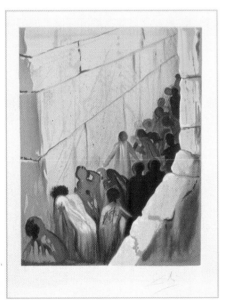

Alyah
1968
25 LITHOGRAPHS
65 X 50 CM

The Bible
1967
105 LITHOGRAPHS
60 X 45 CM

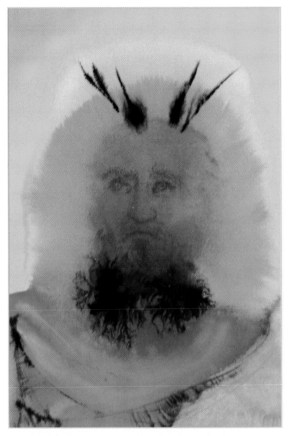

*I am indifferent
to the opinion of others.
The only thing that matters
is that they speak of Dalí,
even if they have
to speak well of him*

Les Douze Tribus d'Israel
1973
12 ENGRAVINGS
50 X 37 CM

Manifeste Mystique
1951
2 ENGRAVINGS
35 X 25 CM

**Moise
et le
Monothéisme**
1974
10 LITHOGRAPHS
AND ETCHINGS
64 X 50 CM

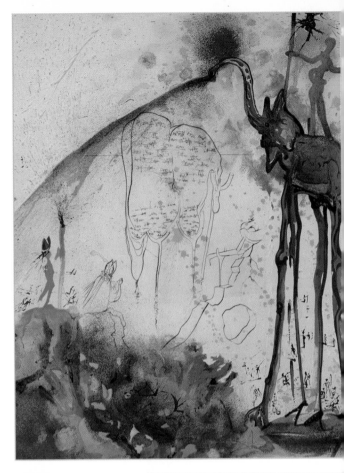

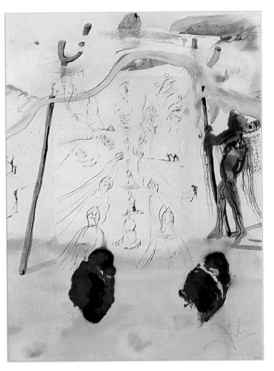

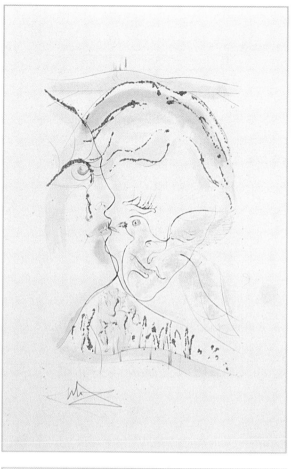

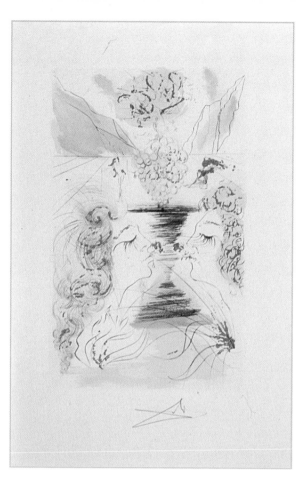

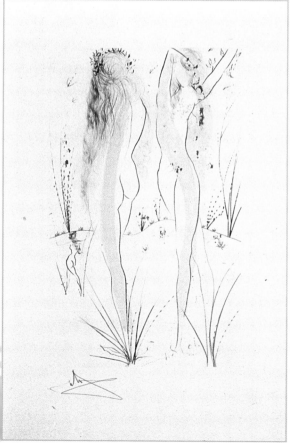

**Song of Songs
of Solomon**
1971
12 COLOUR ETCHINGS
WITH GOLD DUST
40 X 25 CM

**Coronation
de San Salvador d'Orta**
1950
WATERCOLOUR
100 X 75 CM

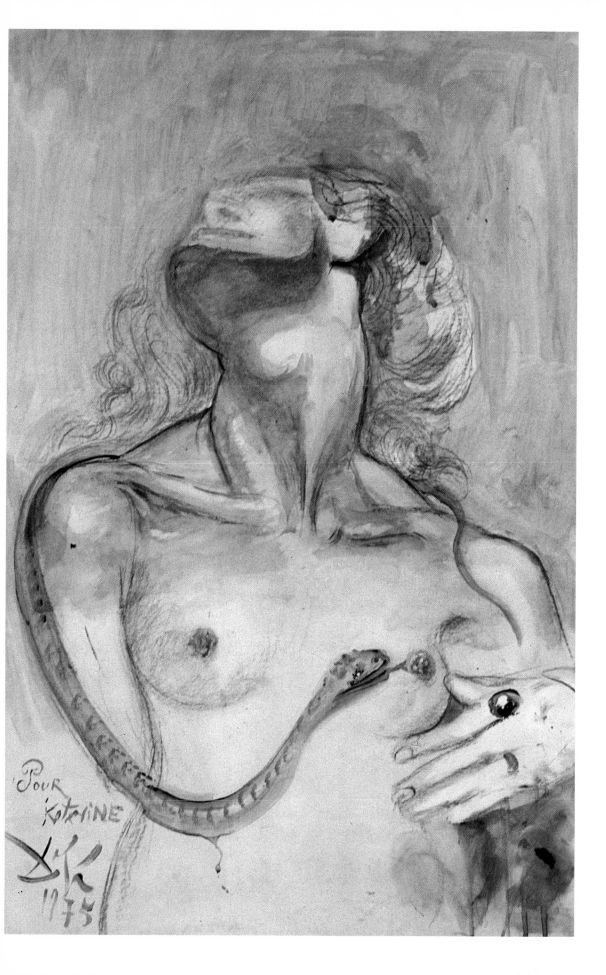

Eve and the Serpent
1975
WATERCOLOUR
49 X 74 CM

BIOGRAPHY

1904

Born in Figueras, Spain on May 11th; first painting, a landscape, is dated 1910.

1914

Begins secondary education at the Marist Brothers' school in Figueras where his interest in painting begins and is influenced particularly by Ramon Pixtox (1872-1925). Most of Dalí's early work is of landscapes and genre scenes of peasants and fishermen.

1918

Interest and experimentation in Impressionism; first canvases are exhibited for local artists held at the Teatre Municipal in Figueras.

1921

Dalí enrolls in the San Fernando School of Fine Arts in Madrid; he meets Lorca, Buñel and Montes and is influenced by the Italian Futurists, Bonnard and Eugène Carrière.

1922

Exhibits at the Galeries Dalmau in Barcelona. In Paris André Breton, together with Picasso, Max Ernst and Man Ray, forms the first Surrealist group.

1923

Arrested for anarchist tendencies and imprisoned for 35 days; interest grows in Cubism and Italian Metaphysical School (Carrà and de Chirico).

1925

First one-man show in Barcelona; Picasso and Mirò show interest in his work; Dalí begins collaboration with Barcelona review "L'Amis de les Arts" which lasts until 1929.

1926

Dalí visits Paris (meets Picasso) and Brussels; is expelled from Fine Arts School; Mirò visits Dalí in Cadaqués; second one-man show at the Galeries Dalmau; interest grows among critics and public.

1927

Dalí does military service; spends summer with Lorca and Regino Sàinz de la Maza; writes poem *Saint Sebastian* which is published in "L'Amis de les Arts".

1928

Lluis Montanyà, Sevastià Gasch and Dalí issue the revolutionary *Yellow Manifesto;* his work is influenced by Mirò, Arp, Ernst, and Tanguy. three of his paintings are shown at the 27th painting exhibition of the Carnegie Institute, Pittsburgh, U.S.A.

1929

Dalí in Paris to work with Buñuel on the film *Un Chien Andalou* which causes a sensation; Mirò introduces Dalí to Surrealist group and is introduced to Magritte, Paul Eluard and Gala, who eventually becomes his wife; Dalí's first exhibition, presented by Breton, at the Galerie Goemans in Paris.

1930

"Le Surréalisme au Service de la Révolution" publishes *Reverie* one of Dalí's most important texts; ten works by Dalí are shown in what should be regarded as the first Surrealist exhibition in the United States; Dalí publishes the text *L'Ane Pourri* where he lays down the foundation of his paranoiac-critical method.

1931

First of three exhibitions which are to be held over the next three years at the Galerie Pierre Colle.

1932

Persistence of Memory arouses enormous curiosity among New York gallery-goers in a group exhibition at the Julien Levy Gallery in New York.

1933

Dalí signs contract with Albert Skira, undertaking to do forty sketches for Lautréamont's *Les Chants de Maldoror*; first one-man show at the Julien Levy Gallery in New York; in December Dalí exhibits at the Galeria d'Art Catalònia, Barcelona.

1934

Exhibitions held at the Salon des Indépendants, Julien Levy Gallery, Galerie Jacques Bonjean, Carnegie Institute, and Zwemmer Gallery in London – his first one-man show in Britain; Gala and Dalí arrive in N.Y. for the first time; lectures at the Wadsworth Atheneum in Hartford, Conn.

1936

The Surrealist exhibition of objects presented at the Galerie C. Ratton in which Dalí participates marks the "officialization" of a new expression of Surrealism; returns to N.Y. and his photo appears on front cover of 'Time' magazine; exhibits at Julien Levy Gallery again and in a collective show at the Museum of Modern Art entitled "Fantastic Art, Dada and Surrealism".

1937

Dalí continues to be widely published, elaborating on the concept of Surrealism; after the murder of Lorca in '36 at the outbreak of the Spanish Civil War, Dalí flees to Italy and is influenced by Renaissance and the Baroque.

1938

Participates in Surrealist exhibition at the Galerie des Beaux Arts in Paris; introduced to Sigmund Freud in London; collaborates with Coco Chanel on several ballet designs for the Ballets de Montecarlo.

1939

New York, exhibition at Levy Gallery; signs contract with N.Y.'s World Fair to create *The Dream of Venus* but encounters differences with its sponsors over his ideas, later when his plan to put a fish's head on Botticelli's *Venus* is prohibited, he publishes his "Declaration of the independence of imagination and of man's right to his own madness"; Dalí designs scenery for first paranoiac ballet *Bacchanal* which is performed at the Metropolitan Opera House; Gala and Dalí return to Europe and settle in Arcachon, and the Spanish Civil War ends with General Franco's victory.

1940

With the onset of World War II, Dalí leaves Europe for Virginia and stays at Caresse Crosby's house; he later settles in Pebble Beach, California; Dalí remain in U.S. until 1948.

1941

Dalí is very successful in America; begins prolific collaboration with photographer Philippe Halsman, which ends with the latter's death in 1979; Dalí finishes his *Secret Life*, published in 1942; Dalí creates libretto, scenery and costumes for ballet *Labyrinth* at Metropolitan Opera House.

1942

Retrospective show at Museum of Modern Art is exhibited in eight other American cities.

1943

Dalí becomes accepted member of New York society; paints portraits of rich Americans for Knoedler Gallery and constructs his famous Mae West's face.

1944

Theatrical activities intensify and begins working on illustrations for many books.

1945

The explosion of the atom bomb at Hiroshima inspires Dalí to begin his "nuclear" or "atomic" period; works with Alfred Hitchcock on the dream sequence in "Spellbound".

1947

Dalí illustrates edition of *Essays of Montaigne* and has one-man show at the Cleveland Museum of Art and later at the Bignou Gallery, N.Y.

1948

Leaves for Europe to settle for good in Port Lligat; exhibits at the Galleria l'Obelisco in Rome; enters into a new phase, in which he has no point of contact with the postwar *avant-garde* but, on the contrary, focuses on the great themes of western tradition.

1949

Designs secenery for Strauss' *Salome* at Covent Garden in London; his interest in harmonic and geometric theory grows; returns to New York.

1950

Dalí publishes book, *Memorandum* as response to his sister's book; designs costumes and scenery for Zorrilla's *Don Juan Tenorio* at the Teatro Maria Guerrero in Madrid; many of his drawings at this time are influenced by religion and mythology.

1952

Dalí explains the elements of nuclear mystique in a seven city tour in the U.S.; is commissioned to illustrate *La Divina Commedia* for the anniversary of Dante, creates 103 watercolours.

1954

Major retrospective of Dalí's work in Rome (Palazzo Pallavicini), Venice and Milan successively.

1958

Initiates 'optical art', seeking optical effects and illusions; Gala and Dalí are married at the 'Chapel of Angels' in Spain; Dalí is presented by the Cuban Ambassador in Paris with the *Médaille à la Qualité Française* for his series of illustrations of *Don Quixote* (1957).

1959

Dalí visits Pope John XXIII.

1960

The Surrealists write the article *We don't hear it that way*, against Dalí's participation in an international exhibition of Surrealism in New York; Dalí begins work on *The World of Salvador Dalí*.

1962

Dalí concentrates increasingly on the main themes of his past career, which he examines and works out again and again; *Dalí de Gala* published.

1963

Exhibition of most recent works at Knoedler Gallery, New York; publication of book *The Tragic Myth of Millet's Angelus* written in 1933.

1964

Dalí is decorated with the Grand Cross of Isabel la Catòlica; publication of *Dairy of a Genius*; major retrospective in Tokyo, Japan organized by Mainichi Newspaper.

1965

The Gallery of Modern Art in New York shows never seen paintings from Reynolds Morse's private collection; Dalí illustrates the *Bible* with 105 watercolours; develops interest in holography and three-dimensional art.

1968

Publication of *Les Passions Selon Dalí* and *Dalí de Draeger*.

1969

Publication of *Las Metamorfosis Eròticas*, one of the high points of his paranoiac-critical method; exhibition at Knoedler Gallery arouses great interest in American press; Dalí announces the creation of the Dalí museum in Figueras; works on commercial poster for such companies as *Perrier, Lanvin* chocolates, and the French Railways; Boymans-van Beuningen Museum in Rotterdam organizes first of the major retrospectives in Europe.

1971

Formal opening of the Dalí museum in Cleveland consisting largely of the Morse Collection.

1973

'Dalínian Holographic Room' is exhibited; Dalí illustrates *Dix Recettes D'Immortalité* and *Roi Je t'attends à Babylone*.

1974

Retrospective at the Stadel Museum in Frankfurt-am-Main; opening of the Dalí Museum-Theatre.

1978

Guggenheim Museum, New York presents Dalí's first hyper-stereoscopic works; Dalí is elected a foreign associate member of the Académie Francaise des Beaux-Arts.

1980

Major retrospective at Tate Gallery, London; Dalí delivers portrait of the King of Spain to the Zarzuela Palace in Madrid.

1981

Dalí recovers slowly from an illness contracted in New York; concerned for his health, Dalí is visited at his house in Port Lligat by King Juan Carlos and Queen Sofia of Spain.

1982

Attends formal opening of the Dalí Museum of St. Petersburg, Florida, founded by Morse; the Honourable Jordi Pujol, President of the Autonomous Government of Catalonia presents Dalí with the Governmental Gold Metal; Dalí's wife Gala dies on June 10th after over fifty years of companionship, and is buried on the grounds of the Castle of Pubol; Dalí's last paintings are made; after losing his wife, Dalí abandons public life and closes himself off in his Castle of Pubol.

1989

Salvador Dalí dies at the age of 84 on January 23rd.

INDEX

MISCELLANEOUS